# Plainsongs

**Editor**

Eric R. Tucker

**Associate Editors**

Becky Faber, Michael Catherwood, Eleanor Reeds

**Editors Emeriti**

Dwight Marsh, Laura Marvel-Wunderlich

**Publisher**

Corpus Callosum Press

Cover photo by Amy Sandeen

Corpus Callosum Press
Hastings, Nebraska

Subscriptions to *Plainsongs* are $25.00 annually for two issues, published in January and July. Subscriptions can be purchased online at the Corpus Callosum Press website.

*Plainsongs* welcomes submissions. The manuscript deadline for the Summer 2022 issue is December 15, 2021. Contributors will receive one free copy of the issue in which their poem appears. For each issue, the Board of Readers will select three poems to be honored as award poems. Award poem winners will receive a small monetary amount, currently $50.

Please use our online submission manager, available at the Corpus Callosum Press website, to submit work. Though we will endeavor to consider all e-mailed and snail-mailed submissions, we cannot guarantee responses for work submitted via these methods. Non-submission correspondence can be e-mailed to etucker@corpuscallosumpress.com or mailed to Corpus Callosum Press, PO Box 1563, Hastings, NE 68902. For more information about submitting poetry or subscribing to *Plainsongs*, please see our website: https://www.corpuscallosumpress.com/plainsongs.

Cover photo by Amy Sandeen.

*Plainsongs* is indexed by Humanities International Complete, EBSCO Information Services, 10 Estes Street, Ipswich, MA 01938.

ISBN-13   978-0-9996869-8-0

ISSN 1534-3820

# Plainsongs

Winner of the Jane Geske Award,
presented by the Nebraska Center for the Book

# Contents

Poetry amid Pandemic: An Interview with Nebraska Poet Kiara Nicole Letcher ...9
Diaper ............................................................................................................12
    *Carrie Jewell*
About "Diaper": A *Plainsongs* Award Poem .......................................................13
    *Michael Catherwood*
To a Friend in Lockdown in Manhattan ..........................................................14
    *Max Roland Ekstrom*
About "To a Friend in Lockdown in Manhattan": A *Plainsongs* Award Poem ......15
    *Eleanor Reeds*
Lipstick ...........................................................................................................16
    *Patricia L. Hamilton*
About "Lipstick": A *Plainsongs* Award Poem ...................................................18
    *Becky Faber*
Out of the Dark Woods ..................................................................................19
    *Michael Catherwood*
Researching Communication Technologies .....................................................20
    *Eleanor Reeds*
On Seeing the Poet Laureate in Target on a Sunday Afternoon .........................21
    *Becky Faber*
The Ghosts Are Hungry ..................................................................................22
    *Kiara Nicole Letcher*
Getting Home from Grand Marais ..................................................................23
    *Scott Lowery*
Estate .............................................................................................................24
    *Marina Greenfeld*
Heap of Wood ................................................................................................25
    *Mark Metcalf*
At the Madison County Covered Bridge Festival .............................................26
    *L. Sweeney*
The Dying of the Light ...................................................................................27
    *Donna Pucciani*
Cheyenne Smith .............................................................................................28
    *Zak Hartzell*
Election Night Roadkill ..................................................................................30
    *John Fritzell*
Public Television .............................................................................................31
    *Adam Tavel*
Inherited ........................................................................................................32
    *Bonny Barry Sanders*
Strangers and Other Friends ...........................................................................33
    *Ken Holland*
Starting from the End ....................................................................................34
    *Robert S. King*
Sheltering in Place ..........................................................................................35
    *Deborah H. Doolittle*

Sleight of Hand Master Ricky Jay & Cornell Professor Carl Sagan Discuss the
Trajectory of Cards on Mars ........................................................................... 36
    *Roy Bentley*
Encounter ............................................................................................................ 37
    *Linda M. Lewis*
Snakes .................................................................................................................. 38
    *Emily Kingery*
Hide ..................................................................................................................... 40
    *Hannah Marshall*
Angst .................................................................................................................... 41
    *George Young*
Summer Says ....................................................................................................... 42
    *Doris Ferleger*
Domesticity ......................................................................................................... 43
    *Amy L. Fair*
Domestic Dream of a Post-Pandemic World .................................................. 44
    *Robert Detman*
Anatomy Lesson ................................................................................................. 45
    *Cristina Legarda*
Meditation .......................................................................................................... 46
    *P M F Johnson*
Vela ...................................................................................................................... 47
    *E. Samples*
Jazz Hand Dancer .............................................................................................. 48
    *R. Steve Benson*
Dulcet Tones Blaming ....................................................................................... 49
    *Kenneth Pobo*
World's Largest Prairie Dog .............................................................................. 50
    *John Wojtowicz*
Berry Picker ........................................................................................................ 52
    *Mary Ann Meade*
Avalanche Lounge .............................................................................................. 53
    *Mario Duarte*
The Hornet Moon .............................................................................................. 54
    *Jack Granath*
A Chaos of Crows .............................................................................................. 55
    *Marilyn Dorf*
Last Things ......................................................................................................... 56
    *Matthew J. Spireng*
A Guide to American Movies in Russian Submarines .................................. 58
    *Ceridwen Hall*
The Paranormal of Stay ..................................................................................... 59
    *Daniel Edward Moore*
Thunderclouds ................................................................................................... 60
    *John Leonard*
The Saving Grace ............................................................................................... 61
    *Paul Ilechko*

A Myth with Many Faces .................................................................62
   *Ivan Hobson*
On the Imagined Floor of the Jeffrey Ward.....................................63
   *Joe Baumann*
Emily's Virtues ..................................................................................64
   *Luci Shaw*
Little Leviathan .................................................................................66
   *Forrest Rapier*
watchclock (12/8) .............................................................................68
   *Xavier Reyna*
Folklore for Missouri Boys................................................................69
   *Kimberly Ramos*
Oscar, Gone Home Now..................................................................70
   *Phoebe Blake*
The Teresa .........................................................................................71
   *Angela Gabrielle Fabunan*
On Edge............................................................................................72
   *Jerrice J. Baptiste*
Plans .................................................................................................73
   *Dana Stamps, II*
Imagination at Reverie Lake ............................................................74
   *Esther Palmer*
The Crepe Myrtle Tree......................................................................76
   *Linda Hughes*
On the last day..................................................................................77
   *s. Nicholas*
parallelogram.....................................................................................78
   *RC deWinter*
Professional Rioters ..........................................................................79
   *José A. Alcántara*
Two Girls in Montana......................................................................80
   *Judith Mikesch McKenzie*
silhouette...........................................................................................81
   *German Dario*
The Man in the Owl Costume.........................................................82
   *Vincent Green*
a harsh environment for our nature .................................................83
   *Emily Jacko*
Protag................................................................................................84
   *grace (ge) gilbert*
The city of diseased appletrees. ........................................................85
   *DS Maolalai*
Autobiography ..................................................................................86
   *Hibah Shabkhez*
Remainder.........................................................................................87
   *Deborah Pope*

Flock ..........................................................................................................88
    *Joey Brown*
Concerning the Illegitimate Son of the Mayor from JAWS: Gov. DeSantis ..........90
    *Christina Fulton*
Legacy ........................................................................................................92
    *Callie S. Blackstone*
Drought ....................................................................................................94
    *Margo L. Foreman*
Rearview: Minnesota ................................................................................95
    *Eve Taft*
Alternate Lives ..........................................................................................96
    *Michael Waterson*
The Final Days of Houdini ......................................................................97
    *Chad Christensen*
Birth Duplex ............................................................................................98
    *Jason A. Terry*
making a map ..........................................................................................99
    *Noël Bella Merriam*
Handwringing Ridges ............................................................................100
    *Lily Rose Kosmicki*
Wash Day ................................................................................................102
    *Mark Rhoads*
Clearing ..................................................................................................103
    *Trivarna Hariharan*
Elizabeth Bishop Reads My Horoscope ................................................104
    *Julia McConnell*
Tattoo Days ............................................................................................106
    *Dale Cottingham*
Scorpinacity ............................................................................................107
    *C. Prudence Arceneaux*
salamander ..............................................................................................108
    *Brendan Walsh*
Bananas ..................................................................................................109
    *Shyla Shehan*
When My Father Looked Up ................................................................110
    *Lucy Adkins*
Deer Beds ................................................................................................111
    *Jack Chielli*
Thirty-Six Zeroes ....................................................................................112
    *Steve Denehan*
Midnight's Fire ......................................................................................114
    *Catherine Stansfield*
Eating the Last Tomato ..........................................................................115
    *Kevin D. Norwood*
Camping with Emily Dickinson ............................................................116
    *William L. Ramsey*

# Poetry amid Pandemic: An Interview with Nebraska Poet Kiara Nicole Letcher

*Kiara Nicole Letcher is a poet residing in Omaha, Nebraska. Her debut chapbook,* Scream Queen, *is available for purchase from Orchard Street Press.*

*First of all, how have you handled writing, working, living, etc., throughout this past year?*

It has been a series of highs and lows. At the beginning of the pandemic I found out I was pregnant with our third baby. Which was so amazing. We also decided to move houses so we had room for everyone. We were getting cramped already in our old home. We had just mentally and physically outgrew that home, so even though the world was kind of wonky it was time for us to move on.

*Many writers have reported that long-term home confinement has not been the kind of boon to creativity that they thought it might be. How has the pandemic affected the ways in which you think about or approach the writing process?*

When the pandemic hit, I was very isolated. Being pregnant is already such a thing to carry physically and mentally, but during the pandemic, it was even more isolating. My writing really took a back seat. I just wasn't in a place mentally to put thoughts into poem format. So I tried to keep reading and watching things that would inspire me. Anytime a poetic thought popped into my head, or I read something that struck me or a friend said something I wanted to remember, I would jot that down. I have a treasure trove of snippets of writings.

*What's your earliest memory of reading and writing poetry?*

Federico Garcia Lorca's "Gypsy Ballads" or "Romancero Gitano" really sticks out for me. Each poem was a spell, a mood, a wish. A trembling of people wounded, in love or bloody.

"Romance Sonámbulo"
Over the mouth of the cistern
the gypsy girl was swinging,
green flesh, her hair green,
with eyes of cold silver.
An icicle of moon
holds her up above the water.

I also really connected with Sylvia Plath in high school. I read anything and everything I could find that she had written and about her. Anne Sexton's "Her Kind" has been in the back of my mind since I first read it in high school and Patricia Smith's "Blood Dazzler" really made an impact on me.

"Katrina"
I was a rudderless woman in full tantrum,
throwing my body against worlds I wanted.
I never saw harm in lending that aches.
All I ever wanted to be
was a wet, gorgeous mistake,
a reason to crave shelter.

*What words would you use to describe your poetic style? How would you say your work as evolved over the years?*

My poems have gotten sharper and more teeth over the years. It's always focused on some angle of horror or myths and has had elements of magic. But in the beginning my writing was a little shy and timid. Over the years it's swelled into something a little braver.

*Can you say a little bit about your creative process? What are some of the things that tend to inspire you? How do you know when an idea or image will become a poem? Do you have a favorite time/place for writing? Sorry, that's a lot.*

I tend to write only at night. Something about ending the day by putting my thoughts into a collection has always been something I loved. Before I had kids I would write all night. I'm for sure more of a night owl than an early bird. Very often I'll have a glass of wine and write from one of the phrases I've jotted down and just start to free write. I like to see where a phrase will take me, what else does it have to say. It becomes a living thing.

I have always been inspired by horror films. I love classic slashers, but also anything moody. I also get ideas from art, music, and media images. I wrote a bunch of poems once based on a video of this actress (Paz de la Huerta) who was just super glamorous and very drunk. The horror and sadness of the video mixed with the glamour lives rent free in my head and inspired a lot of poems.

*How would you describe the experience of writing and publishing your 2019 collection* Scream Queen?

I watched a lot of horror movies and drank a lot of wine, ha! I had a lot to say. There are a handful of poems that were made by just me free-falling into the piece. Those are the ones I like reading the most. I can still feel the energy when I wrote those poems and I hope that comes across when others read the work or listen to me present it.

*The pandemic forced us to cancel our live* Plainsongs *event last April, and you, along with several other poets, were kind enough to share with us a video recording of your reading. Thanks for that! As we begin to emerge from the pandemic, what are some of the things you're looking forward to the most, literary or otherwise?*

Getting together with writers and talking, in person! Going and sitting in a space and hearing other writers' work. There's just something so magical about that!

*What are some of your literary influences? Are there certain poets you find yourself going back to again and again?*

Natasha Trethaway's *Bellocq's Ophelia*, Graham Faust, Zach Schomburg. I love *Scary, No Scary*. Zach was one of my mentors and that is such a strange, solid book. It really helped me see I can lean into the strange.

There is a short horror story called "Cleopatra Brimstone" by Elizabeth Hand that has always stuck with me. I read it in an anthology called *Poe's Children*. I named a poem after the butterfly from the story and there's something that brings me back to that tale frequently.

*What are you reading and/or writing at the moment, or what do you plan to work on in the near future?*

Right now I'm reading more novels. I'm currently reading *Circe*, by Madeline Miller.

I'm starting to piece together the hundreds of small snippets of writing and mini poems. I have an idea where it's taking me but anytime I've thought that, the journey leads somewhere totally different.

*June 2021*

# Diaper

My daughter needed a new diaper
the other night in my dream. She is
seven now, but in the dream she is
sitting on the floor of her room
in the dark, smiling as babies do when
they see their mothers at 2 a.m.

I pick her up, and right away she has
diarrhea, my arms and hands are covered.
Then I'm putting the new, white diaper on,
and it's uncanny how my hands remember
the feeling of the tape pulls, that snug, clean
moment when the diaper is on and sits right
up high over the baby's navel and I give her that
pat on the butt to say, all better, off you go.
When I pick her up to put her back
in the crib, the skin on her arms and
back is softer than water.

It must be the utility of that kind of
touch that I miss. All business, diapering
needs to be done, but in the transition from filthy
to sweet is a river of warm and light.

I remember it now. Even at two a.m.,
I would grit my teeth and admit I'd
miss this, being the baby's
whole pillow, and bath, and earth.

**Carrie Jewell**
**Acton, Massachusetts**

# About "Diaper": A *Plainsongs* Award Poem

In Carrie Jewell's poem "Diaper," imagery and description bring her dream of changing her now seven-year-old daughter's diaper back to the present. Jewell's mater-of-fact tone is contrasted with tender images that infuse the poem with quiet beauty and tenderness.

The mess of changing a diaper "in the dark" night is included in an honest depiction of the task: "right away she has / diarrhea, my arms and hands are covered." Jewell's raw details gives the dream poem force. She then mentions more pleasant imagery: "it's uncanny how my hands remember / the feeling of the tape pulls"; she adds "that… / moment when the diaper is on and sits right / up high over the baby's navel."

The beauty of the simple task completed is profound, profound that six years later the intimacy and care do not need more than the specificity to portray a duty that was repeated hundreds of times. She adds, "When I pick her up to put her back / in the crib, the skin on her arms and / back is softer than water." Tactile imagery guides the dream poem with affection and precision.

Often, poems constructed from dreams can have a surreal angle that can overwhelm a poem. Jewell does not steer her poem in that direction, but instead shares the wonderment that visits her. She explains the duty of "diapering / needs to be done / but in the transition from filthy / to sweet is a river of warm and light."

The speaker's final revelation: she would "miss this, being the baby's / whole pillow, and bath, and earth."

**Michael Catherwood**
**Omaha, Nebraska**

# To a Friend in Lockdown in Manhattan

The first time you got hammered
in the city was with me—I hauled
you from the station in Yonkers
and left you like a boxer in your shoes

flat out in bed, then walked into spring,
fertilizer breathing from campus gardens
and multiplying grubs. Three hundred miles
and two decades later, I watch robins

feast on them after the cold, starless
weeks, soon spotting the first crocus
shoots in the mud, imagining your voice
through the unfamiliarity of this dream

of hollow streets whose colonials
scream at the sky—they want to break
its code of crow and cloud and end
the mass disorder. I've fixed on you

to stop from bleeding into a million stars—
the flickering candles of lives
at the mercy of strangers' breath—
and make an icon of your face.

**Max Roland Ekstrom**
**Essex Junction, Vermont**

# About "To a Friend in Lockdown in Manhattan": A *Plainsongs* Award Poem

The musical comic Bo Burnham's recent special, *Inside*, has been praised by, among others, *The Guardian* as the first example of meaningful art to have emerged from the pandemic. Burnham captures the intense claustrophobia of lockdown and the fracturing of the self that comes from living an entirely digital existence. Over a year ago, the editorial board of *Plainsongs* and, no doubt, many other literary magazines began receiving submissions that reckoned directly with the realities of the COVID-19 pandemic. I ultimately selected this issue's award poem, addressed "To a Friend in Lockdown in Manhattan," because I wanted to celebrate and share a rare example of an occasional poem that crystallizes a shared experience with forcefully specific intimacy, a pandemic poem that moves beyond cliches and the obvious moral to rank with *Inside* as an artwork of the moment that still presents deeply felt universal truths.

Max Roland Ekstrom establishes the relationship between the speaker and their friend as an effect of shared experience not only in time but in space with the opening anecdote about a late night of drinking. The spring grubs then provide a portal from Manhattan to Vermont as, twenty years later, the speaker longs for the absent friend, "imagining your voice" in the "hollow streets" of a community in lockdown. The lyric has always been voiced to music that can no longer be heard. It has also long been our culture's vehicle to address and invoke the absent beloved to whom we cannot speak or write except through a poem. The speaker's despair and isolation is palpable through the houses that "scream at the sky." In order not to become overwhelmed by the threat posed by the virus, described in a strikingly literal image as "the flickering candles of lives / at the mercy of strangers' breath," the speaker has "fixed" on their friend, creating "an icon of your face." As we stare again at the grid of isolated and oddly lit faces on whatever video conferencing tool we're currently using, may we all focus our attention on the person worthy of becoming an icon, the beacon calling to us to connect.

**Eleanor Reeds**
**Hastings, Nebraska**

# Lipstick

My mother always wore the same shade of lipstick,
no matter what: Magnet Red, named as if color
could be an irresistible force, the ultimate come-hither.

Once as a teenager she'd suffered
a severe sunburn, her lips blistering,
a mistake she wouldn't make again.

She never went outside without protection.
During the Great Depression
she spent a hot July picking apricots

and working in the drying sheds,
a relief after trailing her father
and older sister through migrant camps,

sleeping in tents with strangers all around,
her mother and younger brothers
safe in their beds back home.

My aunt varied her lipstick palette,
radiating confidence even though her husband
turned out to be a womanizing louse,

but my mother kept everything simple, subdued, always
makeup-free except for the shade that never altered,
her only other adornment a string of drugstore beads.

That bright red seemed a beacon
when I was small, calling me to the safe harbor
of her skirts. I never asked questions

even after she warned me about men
with a story about a cad in a convertible
who'd beckoned her over and exposed himself.

Not until I was grown did I begin
to see her wound-bright mouth
as an angry slash,

a warning to steer clear,
and realize that years earlier
she'd reversed that magnet's pole.

**Patricia L. Hamilton**
**Jackson, Tennessee**

# About "Lipstick": A *Plainsongs* Award Poem

Beginning a poem with a very specific—and perhaps universal—image is a strong way to draw a reader in. In "Lipstick," by the end of the first line, I was already remembering that my mother always wore the same fragrance (Tigress) and my father always wore Old Spice.

Moving to the second stanza, I realized that this was not a sweet poem of nostalgia. In those three lines, the poet implements words—*suffered, severe, blistering, mistake*—that set the real mood. While the poem begins with cosmetics, it moves on through economic, historical, and sociological concepts—and ends with a lesson in physics.

The development is beautifully crafted. We see the mother's back story as a migrant worker, parallel to the dismal environment of the Great Depression.

The narrator's aunt changes her lipstick colors, a parallel to her husband changing his female companions. However, the narrator's mother "kept everything simple, subdued"—wearing the same shade of lipstick and "a string of drugstore beads." At this point, the reader sees that the poet has taken us beyond the "ultimate come-hither." The sunburn of the mother's youth, the poverty, the migrant work of picking fruit, the "cad" who "exposed himself": all of these elements have taken a toll.

The last two stanzas give us insight into what the red lipstick means. It's not the "irresistible force" as noted in the first stanza or the "beacon…calling me to the safe harbor of her skirts"; it is "a warning to steer clear," the same way a red stop sign tells us to halt. These lines remind me of lines from Edna St. Vincent Millay's "The courage that my mother had"—"The courage that my mother had / Went with her and is with her still / That courage like a rock…."

The last line is perfect for closing this poem—our lesson in physics—that "she'd reversed that magnet's pole." Magnet Red is not for enticement, but "an angry slash/a warning to steer clear," a sad but satisfying end to a powerful poem.

**Becky Faber**
**Lincoln, Nebraska**

# Out of the Dark Woods

Sasquatch at breakfast
orders coffee and a bear claw.
Sasquatch at the racetrack
paddock bets on the number 5,
who wears a pink and gold jersey;
masked throngs
quickly gobble chili dogs.
"Two minutes to Post."

Sasquatch in bed sick,
then in the bathroom bent
over the toilet.           Sasquatch
on his Hayabusa at 179 MPH
in the turns on the Hammer Schmidt.

Now, in the blur of needles,
a stampede of Taxotere,
taste buds destroyed,
fingernails scattered like confetti.

Against the downtown alley walls,
Sasquatch throws no shadows.
He's thin as a hair.
                    The sun
is a wedge of promise
as it scrambles along
the brick streets.

**Michael Catherwood**
**Omaha, Nebraska**

# Researching Communication Technologies

*A poem for Blueberry, past due.*

While the childhood games, or shadow
georgics, at the poetry reading chime out
more doubt than instruction,
I place my hand on your mother's belly
to feel the knocking (*I am here!*)
like clinking pipes on a submerged boat.

It is a May day that will bring you
to the surface. Later, in bed,
I tensed, sighed out Morse Code
- - - —— —— - - -
I sounded it as affirmation:
Yesssssss…. Oh-oh-oh…. Ssssssh.

Was it to begin a life? The life
that should already have begun,
to which I must say "not yet…"
Would one like you as part inside me cry
- - - (*I am here!*) —— —— (*I am here!*) - - -
to the man so distant?

I receive more doubt than instruction.
I think of mothers. Woolf, Winterson.
Women get locked out of
libraries. I didn't. I lock myself out of
what I dare to want inside of

**Eleanor Reeds**
**Hastings, Nebraska**

# On Seeing the Poet Laureate in Target on a Sunday Afternoon

At first I do not see him,
my eyes drawn to his wife whose luxuriant hair provides an aura
   over them
like some holy couple in an Italian painting

She folds dollar bills, tucking them carefully into her wallet
as she turns her face away from the clerk,
away from their white bags marked with concentric red circles

Their smiles find each other

His hands are cupped in front of him,
a flock of words and memories
nesting between his idle fingers
until they migrate to paper

to tell the story of his father's store,
of his mother's thriftiness,
of the path that today brings him to Target

**Becky Faber**
**Lincoln, Nebraska**

## The Ghosts Are Hungry

The ghosts are hungry
for story.

Tell them of the melodrama
swollen with blood and lamplight.

That time you tried so hard not to cry
your face became a bruise of vermilion and violet.
Like an evening aching to rain.

They said, they said, he said.
    "Your mouth is always open
    in laughter or a tearing yell."

YOU! Split open like
sacred geometry and it was all
too damn much!

Someone pointed to you floating—
Over
    sunset
above

        bonfire.

**Kiara Nicole Letcher**
**Omaha, Nebraska**

# Getting Home from Grand Marais

those nights, in & out of dreams,
I heard black surf break
granite into a clatter
of round gravel

all night, the lake hammered
itself to bronze, thinner
& thinner: a mirror
at sunrise

then today, we lifted & fell
inside the car's tight hull,
our thoughts separate
as skipped stones

tonight, darkened rows of corn
stretch in every direction,
dry waves pounding
on a locked door

**Scott Lowery**
**Rollingstone, Minnesota**

## Estate

The dam. The water throwing itself away—
no wonder she lost track of time.

I screw myself together every morning. A tool
to pull this place apart. A life's rubble sorted—

teacup teacup teacup. I leave the dog biscuits
in the closet for the mice; the dog is gone,

and they were in this house before me.
They'll be here after too. And the constant rush

of the river—there's a child dancing in the hallway,
she says, she has lots of papers to grade. We answer

the phone too much: she's dying, they're going to kill her,
we'll go to hell for what we've done. I leave the window

open to feel my toes slip away. All night long ice
melting in the current. One morning a kingdom

of larvae hatch out of the rug. I follow one blind squirm
to another and another until I see them all. I'm sorry

they were born in such a wrong place. Two in a jar
on the counter to see what they might grow into—

nothing. The last of a bloodline, and their corpses
so small the jar looks empty. My skin feels

like it's crawling away. What will it become
when it's not stuck to me?

**Marina Greenfeld**
**Carrboro, North Carolina**

# Heap of Wood

Not fire, but ice,
abetted by remorseless wind
brought down green ash.
I reduce it to chunks
of trunk and branch,

to stems. And pulling off
opposing twigs for kindling,
build what could probably suffice,
centuries ago, to convert
a heretic to ash.

At what merciful point—
after unnatural curlings and burstings—
did the central nervous system
of the personality on fire
shut down?

At what merciless point—
before the artificial sentence and ignition—
did the central nervous systems
of those insisting on and eyeing the fire
shut down?

**Mark Metcalf**
**Sutton, Nebraska**

# At the Madison County Covered Bridge Festival

we nosh on mushroom burgers from the Hitchin' Post
    while a group of bikers across the park
        congregate
            as if praying.

You gripe about the dirt on your Vette
    while I tease,
        "It's Iowa what do you expect?"

At the Roseman Bridge we read sweet nothings,
    carved or in marker: *27 years after our first kiss*
        *God brought us together.*

        *I will win you back.*

            *F love!*

You laugh,
    These people have no idea what love takes.
        Have they seen the movie?

I know you want to read:
    *Thanks for putting sugar in my coffee.*

"Thanks for being my levity," I say
    then grab your collar,
        "But I don't need you to make me happy
            just don't rain on my bridge!"

*Mutha Fukcah you need Jesus*, the graffiti says,
    and we laugh again before we read:

*Come my love the best is yet to be and let's be together in eternity.*

We pick up some strawberry rhubarb jam
    and cinnamon honey.
        I swish my butt and you say,
            That makes my wiggle tickle.

We don't make it to the Hogback Bridge.

**L. Sweeney**
**Carbondale, Illinois**

# The Dying of the Light

The lengthening shadows
filter through the treetops,
lighting the lawns
like Rapunzel's tresses,
a ladder for the prince
to climb the castle walls.

As a child, I'd lie head down
on the sofa, letting my hair
hang to the floor,
pretending to be a princess.
I wanted my dun-colored curls
to turn ochre for a prince.
I wanted to be older.

My mother told me,
*Don't wish your life away,*
and later, exhausted
by the working life, longing
for weekends and sleep,
I'd think of her words.

A man came to stay,
and together we climbed
the tower of domesticity,
made a castle of the intimate
from the ordinary. Would we
want to be young again?

Too hard the past,
love and labor pulling us
into the future. The mixed blessings
of age are the wisdom of fading skies,
aching bones. The light recedes
by inches, touching the yellow dahlias,
their last sighs dipping, like the sun,
behind the houses.

**Donna Pucciani**
**Wheaton, Illinois**

# Cheyenne Smith

says something by the ticket counter to a boy she calls johnny
finger guns the railroad workers outside the door
maneuvers onto a bench beside me
and perches on the metal mesh.
It's eroded some
with gum clung beneath it
so she eyes Atlanta on a mound of Big League Chew.

We're each in ready position
for a second big bang or a bus or for god to come back with a gun
    this time
silent beside the vending machines
as johnny gambles a buck twenty on sunflower seeds
and the Braves implement aggressive strategies in the ninth
and me too as I spin a tobacco-stained map
striking out a route in the bowels of another greyhound station.

We bloom darkly from Atlanta and Peachtree
where weeds break concrete
sprout up from below and smirk at the homeless—
where Cheyenne Smith has come who taught music
who ruled Seattle whose pale arm once bloomed
below the milky surface in a third-story studio apartment,
Whose mother said *give that boy your number!*
on the steps after rehab
but I have no phone

no number, no name
since johnny hip checked the machine
cajoled an extra bag of Planters and left for Tampa
since the Reds beat the Braves
like divine bullies beating up on boys to build men
and send them lurching forth from shared tenements on the
    outskirts

Men who come here to drive spikes for ten hours
holler at Cheyenne who winks
and hump it past this station again,

spitting into bottles of Coca-Cola
their hopeless seeds
like filthy curses heard young
and sung through the ages
like bones of birds
or a bad taste that just don't
bear mentioning.

**Zak Hartzell**
**Columbus, Ohio**

# Election Night Roadkill

This morning you wake up
and your early-rising wife tells you
that the rabid coon is finally dead,
still warm according to your Lab's inspection,
but bled-out and belly-up on the road out back.
It is late autumn, the worms and grubs buried,
the slough's sushi well-hidden or frozen-
over, every last leaf stripped-down,
scratched-out,
the nails of tendril fingers exposed,
spines stiffened, tremors taut.
All is guilty as charged
by the hard gray etch of November.
A lone crow is perched on the tip-top of the spruce leader,
his call to the carcass amplified
by the cold light air,
echoed by his friends
on their way.

**John Fritzell**
**Appleton, Wisconsin**

## Public Television

the caught gosling chirps
waning in the vixen's
mouth as six starved kits
crowd insensible leaping

its plump yellow tuft
falls and we zoom in to see it
torn open like a goddess
cursed inside her own fable

summer the Arctic greener
than a ball field the narrator
drifts to the gaggle fleeing
on the quicksilver river

who glide the question marks
of their necks spritzed
and glistening impossible
to tell if this is their grief

or animal amnesia that binds
them shivering as they fade
to clots inside a vein beneath
the glacier's broken teeth

**Adam Tavel**
**Quantico, Maryland**

## Inherited

Passed down, folded in the small trunk from Holland,
attic-preserved over sixty years, forgotten.
This quilt covers us now with centenarian warmth.
Hand stitches, small, and as regular
as any sewing machine. Strong threads hold together
a geometry of red and white checks as precise
as the quilted fields outside town. Now it inspires
the landscape of our room—
          comforts us.

Consider the patience of that thimbled finger,
her wish to make something useful and lovely,
her precision of mind alert to balance and form.
Theme and variation inhabit the design
as in classical music. Her story speaks through line,
structure, balance of color, an eye for composition.
It will stay our lives.
          It votes for all that is human, original.

We've inherited an art form that suggests the immortal.
An ancestor's gift—we've always had it and will pass it on.
We lie awake smelling the faintness of muslin
from earth's flax and red dye from secret
German formulas. We fall asleep under beauty
that cannot recall its creator
          avoids its own name.

**Bonny Barry Sanders**
**Jacksonville, Florida**

## Strangers and Other Friends

A friend of mine said to me that on this day of days
He felt the touch of autumn

    Imagine being touched in such a way

A season's pearlescent finger crooks forth
From some cave
        brushes your sleeve

Causes you to turn, and in turning
        the season draws itself away

    Apologizes

Says it mistook you for someone else
        but isn't that what all the seasons say?

And as the season shies back, shies back to shade
        you call it out, you call it out by name.

**Ken Holland**
**Fishkill, New York**

## Starting from the End

Where the road home dead-ends,
only the wind goes on
through the parting grass,

goes on, goes back
like the quantum minds
of children whose dreams
swing high, whose jaws
squeak with nursery rhymes,
whose yawns lullaby
into an ocean of time.

Older eyes stop at the near
horizon, do not see the sun
sail off the edge into open space.

In a possible world,
trees travel far on roots and wind.
Tied to a swaying branch,
I would go along, sail or fall
with autumn leaves.

From a distant limb ahead
a tire swing creaks,
and laughter that could be mine
is flying there.

**Robert S. King**
**Athens, Georgia**

## Sheltering in Place

This is not about brook trout
or mountain cascades.

There will be no laurels for the pine trees
or those pioneers who cut them

down to size. You will not see
the lone cabin tucked inside the wood,

nor the curl of smoke tickling the longleaf,
bristlecone needles like a feather.

You will not be disturbed by infinite,
inclement weather.

There are no hurricanes predicted
for your unforeseen future.

No fire brigades or renegade cops
as you cling to what you got.

You crawl into bed, plump that pillow,
know all of this is in your head

and all those things you have said
can't be unsaid.

**Deborah H. Doolittle**
**Jacksonville, North Carolina**

# Sleight of Hand Master Ricky Jay & Cornell Professor Carl Sagan Discuss the Trajectory of Cards on Mars

*To the ancient Greeks and Romans, the known world comprised Europe and an attenuated Asia and Africa, all surrounded by an impassable World Ocean. Travelers might encounter inferior beings called barbarians or superior beings called gods.*
    Carl Sagan, *Pale Blue Dot*

If Ricky Jay believes in a pure joy of endless hours of practice,
shuffling reshuffling until the clubs diamonds spades hearts fade,
Carl Sagan likes quoting Marcus Aurelius on the relational size
of the Pale Blue Dot, preaching that all plant and animal life
is stardust. If they meet in the middle, grandly showboating,

it's misdirection wisely plotted then gloriously spontaneous.
Ricky Jay isn't much of a student, and Cornell is no circus.
There are stage lights and shadows against the stage curtains:
two Rickys and two Carls doing the math, showing their work,
forecasting the flightpaths of playing cards on Mars. Carl Sagan

posits the atmospheric variables, handing off to Ricky who begins
throwing the auxiliary deck into a watermelon half, piercing a green
pachydermous outer hide with the one-eyed jacks, the Jack of Spades
and the Jack of Hearts abutting on the round fruit skin. After applause,
Cornell professor Sagan describes the trajectory of the human future as

stagecraft so white-knuckle thrilling it might as well be prestidigitation.
Ricky Jay's shoulder-length black hair flies out as he applauds Sagan
who will never see him as the dice man Eddie Sawyer in *Deadwood*,
sporting a three-piece suit and vest and spit-shined dress shoes,
the mustached mechanic of the skill set to say: I've got this.

**Roy Bentley**
**Pataskala, Ohio**

## Encounter

With the entitlement of leviathan, a behemoth
blade for a wind turbine surges past. I glance out
the window of my compact to observe its gargantuan
      passing      passing      passing
as it swims up the river of highway that is I-35.
In the Midwest we often sight them, strapped
on oversized truck and trailer like a sperm whale
lashed to Ahab's Pequod, tapered fluke dipping
to the rhythm of semi wheels slapping pavement.
They travel in pods of three, the shimmering
whiteness of their backs and bellies stark against
atmospheric waves of Kansas-blue sky.

**Linda M. Lewis**
**Lindsborg, Kansas**

## Snakes

I walk alone too much in graveyards
and prairie grass. There could be snakes

hidden low in the cattails, behind pillars
of granite erected before they were

born, pulsing their fists like stomachs until
my tied-up hair swings into view. Sometimes

a snake ripples over the path, it's true, but I
don't startle. There is no goodness in me, or

grace enough to recall the girlish ways of
becoming a mouse. Translucent skin, visible

heart, body near weightless in any man's
important hands. They never hid their jaws'

unhinging, their cold blood and changing
skin in tattoo parlors, and it must be said

I loved them, and it must be said a sacrifice
is not a thing that loves. A mouse never lies

beneath trees and promises power to men,
or flicks in their ears the lie *you will not die*

when their funerals have been arranged.
They say you can know a snake by its skin,

but I know them by starvation. No rush
of birds will warn you if they come close,

no sound of squealing or bones in teeth
or bones in the remains you can keep

as souvenirs. They destroy small, fragile
lives and leave their ghosts: transparent

likenesses of younger, living things. I am
animal, here, filling a well of sour-sweet

venom under my tongue. I know how
it ends for all of us, how the seraphim

who won't touch our kingdom will weep
in gladness when their own is safe.

**Emily Kingery**
**Davenport, Iowa**

# Hide

*I cut off my head and threw it in the sky. It turned into birds. I called it thinking.*
    Richard Siken

Perhaps I could cut open my hide, scrape away flesh
to the birds inside. What feathers would flood the sky?
I am birds in thought; no, thoughts are winged—
I fly, trail eucalyptus and peppermint; I have a head cold
and my birds are wild in the fog.

What would I miss, cleaned to pure thought?
Drinking water from a Mason jar.
The throb of a canker sore.
Diffusing oils beside my desk: cedarwood, thyme, and patchouli.
Illuminated manuscripts.
Covering a hole in the window screen with duct tape.
Geranium flowers.
Road tar, soft in summer.
The light trapped in broken bottles.
Taking out the trash on Tuesday night.

On my walk in the afternoon,
I nod to the large black frog
on a rock by the drainage stream. I wish for him to jump in,
but leave him his peace.
The lilacs are nearly blooming. Quince and cherry.

The birds clamber. My skin stays drawn,
my umbrella, my links of chain.
There is enough, even on this day,
to keep me together, my hand
flexed to caress heart-shaped leaves, to sort
dead maple leaves from the new growth of the hostas.

**Hannah Marshall**
**Grand Rapids, Michigan**

# Angst

   i
There is a loneliness
in the night sky. The stars
are sometimes disturbing to look at—
like the lights
of a strange city spread out below
the wing of your airplane
on approach—
and no one
waiting to meet you.

   ii
Last night, being eighty in the time of
coronavirus, in my dream I once again stumbled
along the dirt path overgrown with grass
on the very edge
of Ireland's Cliffs of Moher (exactly like
Kierkegaard's description: "a place of dread")
where so many souls have slipped and fallen to the rocks
and ocean below. O vertigo.
And I must keep on walking.

   iii
When the hungry man-eating tiger,
drinking
from a still pool of water
in the jungle,
slowly
raises its massive head
and looks at you with remorseless yellow eyes—
what mattered before doesn't
matter anymore.

**George Young**
**Boulder, Colorado**

## Summer Says

Pay attention to
your heat, your survival—
the tree rooted in your garden

is a sequined vernacular, a cashmere sweater.
Because nothing matters in the end
but comfort and the bending light.

Summer says, I will be the room you die in.
You will dream, neither of regret,
nor in the language you were born into.

A stranger will comb your existential threads.
You had thought, for instance, humans
were gerunds or harps bent

on playing in a diner that serves
black coffee and hard donuts.
You ask, *What is the past?*

*What is it all for?*
Summer says, The wound of being
untaught. Says, hungry.

Says, the cypress is a hospice,
says, falter, falter, falter,
bloom bloom bloom—too soon

a pall will keep you company.

**Doris Ferleger**
**Wyncote, Pennsylvania**

# Domesticity

This is not some lackluster
manufactured drama, some
situation spun from boredom
or gloom
or a desire
to fill your Wednesday night
with the same, terse brand
of patience you offer
me, chin cocked.

I am not silently crying
into my housecoat's collar
or filling my apron's calico
pockets to their rickrack brim
with smooth, wet rocks.
Instead, I trimmed back
the flowering basil today, watered
the mesclun, filled a worn basket
with four varieties of heirloom
tomatoes and late-blooming strawberries.
You mowed our grass, walked
our old dog, washed our car.

You've taken out the trash
all your life—
I assume when it's time,
you can do it again.

**Amy L. Fair**
**Winston, Oregon**

# Domestic Dream of a Post-Pandemic World

There used to be consolations,
but the further entrenched and
settled we are, the less do they
console. Imagine this scenario

we all get our just deserts in
the unjust desert. No one raises
a voice or a finger or a child for
that matter. No one is obligated

or under duress in this alternative,
post-pandemic world. And neither
do we clutch to our somnambulant
gods while we cry out in the night,

one lantern among us on this creaking
boat while our ship, the motherlode,
subsumes quietly into the vacuous
dark pool of memory. Instead we float

up in our bubbles, gently jostling but
bringing all to saccharine laughter
and delight bathed in celestial light, not
thinking about tomorrow, not thinking.

**Robert Detman**
**Oakland, California**

## Anatomy Lesson

My cadaver in med school had no breasts
so I named her Saint Agatha. She was old,
very old, and we kept her face covered
for almost the entire dissection. There are things
I will not forget about the anatomy lab:
how Agatha's skin was wrinkled and brown;
the recurrent laryngeal nerve's graceful loop
inside her throat (cut open); Calvin scratching
the tip of his nose on my scrub-clad shoulder
because his gloved hands were covered in muck;
and how I would make up stories about the body,
our "first patient," as we were told to think of her.
I wondered, for I had not yet learned to discern,
if she had had children, or if she'd even had sex.
(Everyone has a sex life, right?) Did she experience
that ecstasy everyone wants, that throbbing joy
that makes us feel so connected? That intimacy
of knowing someone and being known?
Did she ever have a one-night stand
and know the exhilaration of total indifference?
Did she dance when no one was looking,
or laugh a lot (over what?), and did those hands
weave or weld metal or sculpt nudes
out of clay? But most of all I wanted to know
did she feel that terrible pain in her chest,
the one that stabs your heart with a scalpel
right before your tears start to fall?
I was so determined to find that bundle of nerves
I was sure must reside in the thorax, the one that surely
sends electric signals upward so fast, so abominably fast,
the minute a friend says a careless word, or a lover ignores,
or a child hurls venom, or an insult makes landfall.
Where was it? Where was it, that transponder of pain?
I don't know why I thought I would find it there.
Even with her heart in my hands, I was none the wiser;
Even with my heart in yours, nor are you.

**Cristina Legarda**
**Boston, Massachusetts**

# Meditation

That pleasant lack
of thought, that
loss of gotta
as I discard what
runs fast as a fever
rat through my head.
Peace. The precise
moment days of strain
and tension resolve
and the bed awaits.
That sort of silence.
That grace. But inside,
my thoughts spread
like upended bourbon,
like a recent litter
of kittens, like
political certainty.
I want to say I'm
getting better at this,
but there's always
the drum beat somewhere,
the cast hook, a new splash
of glitter across the floor.
What can anyone do?
Return to the mantra,
nothing more. Then
another ring at the door.

**P M F Johnson**
**Minneapolis, Minnesota**

## Vela

Dusting off Dad's old collegiate Webster's
I find dried leaves pressed between
**stamineal** and **stanhope**.
Rows of small type contrast beneath,
cushion and define each carved notch.
Holding an arboreal souvenir to the light
reveals its windrose network;
1960s green, elder web of frequencies
intersecting bookplate ink and fading:
*1213 6th Ave, Apt. 1*
*Huntington, West Virginia*

The dictionary's binding is decrepit.
I navigate clumsily
and the front cover slackens;
Pages flail, flap,
helplessly earthbound.
Unable to avoid a fray
papers splinter and spill
dog-eared trails and retired words.
Whispered vowels scatter
shipwrecked on the floor,
wither like lilies tossed
on a graveyard mound.

**E. Samples**
**Jeffersonville, Indiana**

## Jazz Hand Dancer

Folding clothes together laughing
in a laundromat he began dancing
to Chuck Berry from a radio she
naturally couldn't hear because
she hadn't heard any sounds her
first 35 years here which is why she
surprised him by rising quickly
smiling at him watching her gracefully
focusing her coordination-soul-energy
not on Chuck Berry (she wrote in a note
to him later) but on what she imagined
music might feel like in her muscles,
bones, feet, legs, head and everything
between in this very public scene
where tangled clothes tumbled together
spinning in coin-fed barrels with
glass portholes reflecting their
dancing not touching, her hands
flowing fluidly slightly above
her body's curves and rhythms
spelling feelings gliding over
thighs hips sides chest neck face
long black hair then gracefully
smoothing it back down where
she's shaping warm wet air dancing
freely interpreting emotionally
breathing healthy openly hungry
for more pleasures from her body-
coordination-soul-energy
moving gracefully bravely
focusing her thoughts closing
her eyes then opening them this
self-described "Jazz Hand Dancer"
soundlessly limber in a laundromat
reflected in every silent porthole
shaking and washing whatever is in it.

**R. Steve Benson**
**Mt. Vernon, Iowa**

## Dulcet Tones Blaming

For messing me up,
I don't blame
my parents or
their parents or
their parents.
Or Adam and Eve.
Snakes can be persuasive
when you're naked.
I don't blame the snake,
a chatty little guy.
Should I blame DNA?
A sperm and an egg
make a mess and soon
I'm in third grade,
Mrs. Olaf demanding
that I spell frostbite,
which I get wrong—
she looks like the roof
caves in on her permanent.

What is permanent?
Things keep moving away.
I follow after.

**Kenneth Pobo**
**Media, Pennsylvania**

# World's Largest Prairie Dog

> ...*prairie dogs have alarm calls containing descriptive information about the general size, color, and speed of approaching predators.*
>     Dr. Con Slobodchikoff, Biology Professor and Prairie Dog Linguist, North Arizona University

The twelve-foot pink and ochre likeness
sends drivers skirting off Exit 131
for Cactus Flat, South Dakota,
where potato-sized denizens
of a black-tailed prairie dog town
pop like Whac-a-Moles from burrow mounds.

Ninety-eight percent of the North American
population met the buffalo's fate
when settlers claimed the plains
but here pups are playful,
gossiping above ground.

Prairie dog linguists can distinguish
different high-pitched yipping calls
for *tall human in a yellow shirt*
and *short human in a green shirt.*
*Human with a gun* and *without.*

In the statue's vicinity, their burrows
are protected, exquisite networks
of tunnels and chambers: bedrooms, bathrooms,
and nurseries. Prepared visitors
pull baby carrots from coolers.
Peanuts can be purchased for fifty cents.

What must the black-tails make
of their concrete patron saint?
Do salt-and-pepper elders tell
how under The Great One's spell
humans present gifts
in repentance for the era of killing contests?

Guests aim cameras and shoot
as prairie dogs jump-yip at the sight
of *medium humans in white*
after Labor Day. It's easy to love
those who eat from the palm of your hand.

**John Wojtowicz**
**Bridgeton, New Jersey**

## Berry Picker

Crossing the berry field, I look for a footprint
and then another. *Where did I go?* Did I not
pick bucket after bucket of sweet berry.
Did I not bend to the earth, hear in the wind
*O taste and see.* Slowly, I cross the turn row,
sit in the faded light of evening. Far off
the ring of cow bell, goat bell, all of evening
in sudden praise. Would that I, a picker,
could taste the berry sweetness, caked in the
lifeline of my hand. I rise, follow the road
back to the city where now in winter, I join
the other pickers: the pigeon, the beggar,
the street cleaner. At a stoop, I pick
at bits of stale bread or paper or string.
Most days, I rub the berry stain deeper
into the lifeline of my hand. Other days,
I mutter to the beggar *O see*, drop the stone
of a dried berry in his cup. The truth is
I have a quarry of stone, there in my room
above the deli, the crack in each stone
but bearing the light of the berry field.
In such light, my hands find comfort.
My hands find rest.

**Mary Ann Meade**
**Lansdowne, Pennsylvania**

## Avalanche Lounge

Are we thirsty for the truth?
Why not drop tainted quarters
into the slot for Stevie,
buried in her landslide.

We listen, something missing,
yet manage to pour ourselves
into a shot glass, flaring
into a blue-hearted fireball.

Later, after closing time,
we collide with a masseuse
to a cacophony of thanks
after she kneads the kinks out.

At noon, hungover, thirsty,
we sleepwalk to our old booth,
head down on the sticky table,
a lost nation, lost people.

To the cracking of pool balls,
collisions and rolls into holes,
we dream of an avalanche,
miles of snow, ice and rock,

dream of a sheer red blouse,
or a black t-shirt with red hearts,
unable to breath, eyes closed,
feeling sorry for no change.

**Mario Duarte**
**Iowa City, Iowa**

# The Hornet Moon

Bear it, the sting
of this white wisp,
the hornet moon

that bounces free
unsteadily,
its cloud undone,

parted, let fall,
kicked off, and all
to stab someone,

to find a way
straight through the eye
to brain and bone.

This work is hard—
the moon's bright barb
and you, alone.

**Jack Granath**
**Shawnee, Kansas**

# A Chaos of Crows

Sudden,
a chaos of crows
cawing, hurrahing,
fierce workings of wings
as if the whole world
were suspended,
upended,
over the package
of Cheetos
a village boy spilled
running home from school,
those flavors of cheese,
that crunching of yellow,
flickering spangly as stars
in the deep of
the night.

**Marilyn Dorf**
**Lincoln, Nebraska**

# Last Things

Buy a pair of work boots
in your twenties and you're
sure to wonder whether

next time you need work boots
you'll buy a different brand
because these won't wear well,

or, even if they do,
time will pass and, as with
all things, they'll just wear out

and need to be replaced
and maybe the next pair
will be better. But buy

a pair of work boots in
your seventies and you
might find yourself thinking

this pair will be the last
you buy—that these boots will
last a lifetime, or what's

left of a lifetime. Once
an old guy who checked on
my house while I went on

vacation left a pair
of work boots at the top
of my cellar stairs, boots

to wear when he went down
in the wet basement to
check the furnace and they

did survive him when he
died relatively young
of a heart attack. Now,

the work boots I have that
I bought the year I turned
seventy thinking they

could be my last pair of
work boots are starting to
age, I noticed today

when I came in the house
after carrying wood
from a wet, muddy field

at the edge of the woods
where I'd cut a few trees.
I began wondering

whether I'll have to buy
yet another pair and
whether that pair will be

my last or whether I'll
continue to age well
and will be cutting and

splitting firewood into
my eighties and perhaps
will just drop dead—like the

friend of my parents who
died many years ago
while she was raking leaves

at eighty—one day while
I'm cutting or splitting
wood, die, as they would say

in old Westerns I watched
on TV when I was
a kid, with my boots on.

**Matthew J. Spireng**
**Kingston, New York**

# A Guide to American Movies in Russian Submarines

    The first catastrophe is atmosphere and drill—
        choked, urgent. Compartments flood or burn
    like dominoes. We learn how small their hatch,
            our margin for error, human and mechanical.

Then, a bureaucratic interlude, some floating ideology;
    how ill-equipped and untrained Soviet crews were
for disaster, how in-denial. But by now we think

    we can trust the Russian captain; he reads
        the Bible or, better, novels—he's an American
    actor on an undersea *Millennium Falcon*, with dials to
    monitor,
          records to break. She rolls and plummets, evading

a danger. Inside, they drop subtitles and heavy accents, speak
    so the audience can eavesdrop. We're all alike underwater;
things blur and echo. Music fades to an ominous thrum

    as the requisite *zampolit* lectures and sailors pretend
        to listen. Sooner or later, a young officer checks
    the periscope to find the enemy, our navy,
           eyeing him. They dive, turbines strewing bubbles,

and our scale is flipped: the boats are toys on wires.
    Inside men rush down ladders. Mere inches divide
the ocean and their whispers about risk versus duty.

    As for the sub, it will take two hours—a few watches
        condensed—to scuttle or to save her with the crew,
    who pretend, as we do, not to know how, if,
           each crisis is resolved. Meanwhile, we hear
           commands

ignored or obeyed. Perhaps, in this story, we manage to defer
    annihilation, for ourselves—our enemies, until the credits
        roll.

**Ceridwen Hall**
**Cincinnati, Ohio**

# The Paranormal of Stay

If summer taught us anything
it begins by digging holes.

Hard, like the heart
pumping a shovel
with fuel into wrinkled hands.

It is almost supernatural,
watching perennial pull the pin
on a lovely tulip grenade.

The way morning's whip
of light trains
the ground with color.

You could not recall
the last time words
painted eyes with petals

which is why you bought
season tickets for
the paranormal of stay.

**Daniel Edward Moore**
**Oak Harbor, Washington**

# Thunderclouds

Our baseline was fog and blur, seven hundred days of rain or
 without rain.
Both ways were bad for your neighbor's ailanthus and the sky
 became
the same color as scar tissue on a narwhal. What have you done
to find yourself in a pawn shop on Sunday morning, right before
 church?

You don't know me anymore—a sidewalk closed off to pedestrians
so that fire ants can finish their meal of a dead Persian Gray.
When the phone rang, I didn't want to disrupt myself
from dredging bird nests out of our gutters. Music suckled

at the air like static and my father's lungs were blinking rapidly.
The first day in June, just before storm season, while his tackle box
sat cloistered on a mossy creek bed somewhere in eastern
 Mississippi.
We forget things and that's how we forget people. But we never
 forgot this:

How both of our grandmothers pulled out our baby teeth with
 ardor
and a rusted fear that our hands would get dirty from drool and
 blood.
Now, we ask ourselves if sunshine is rare like a crucifixion or a
 second coming,
and the cross above the bowling alley just seemed off today.

**John Leonard**
**Elkhart, Indiana**

# The Saving Grace

The width of a line would vary
depending on the pressure of the stroke

a thick black line that still contained
the smolder from the burn          a triggering

flame that ended with an action of
retorsion          savagery preceding savagery

the line as an edge          as a bladed darkness
a jagged saw that separates and severs

all connection    the others now all gone
they've been removed from here

extracted          and sent on down a curving
track     until they reach the burning border

drained of all vitality       asemic yet
significant         the painful scars are scratched

into the surface of a life   it's all destruction
leave us with your pictograph

your metaphoric scribble that extricates
us from anxiety's furnace.

**Paul Ilechko**
**Lambertville, New Jersey**

# A Myth with Many Faces

The newly minted blue-collar retiree
does nothing but sit in his home
and after three months, or six months,
(never longer than two years) is found dead
clutching a television remote control.

In another version, the dead retiree is found
clutching a *Vogue* or *Cosmopolitan* magazine,
something he would have never read
except in despair and loss of masculinity.

In yet another version, the dead retiree is found
(again no longer than two years from retirement)
clutching a smart phone, not in an attempt to call 911,
but in an attempt to purchase something
like a brocade holiday-outfit for his dog or cat.

This common blue-collar myth, working
to showcase the price of retirement as death.
Every version I have heard involves *clutching*,
as though somehow a blue-collar heart
is not found in the chest, but rather in the hands.

And every version I have heard also includes a man,
typecast and burly until he wilts in retirement;
as though his calories really came from hard labor,
his brand of manliness from the tools he possessed.

Maybe the myth started as a dream of Henry Ford:
that all workers would voluntarily forgo pension
and retirement for fear of death. Maybe we workers
started it all—a myth to keep us from regretting
all the beautiful things we were missing at home.

**Ivan Hobson**
**Martinez, California**

# On the Imagined Floor of the Jeffrey Ward

I stood beneath the tower where
my sister prayed for oranges
to rain down
spiked with cloves so everything
would smell like Christmas, that
anise-infused aroma of
new beginnings and stockings and
coal that isn't ever lit.

I was alone and washed in
light, bioluminescent, neon, scented with
pine and mouthwash.

Really
it was not a tower but a conundrum
of machinery, beeping and snoring out
commands—
or, well, not commands but responses to
her heartbeat
her breath
the ebbing strength of the blood that rippled through
her vena cava.

She had, by then, become nothing more
than the slow churn of a kiddie pool.

Her voice was parchment paper, scraped ragged by
the pen of her worry. She was concerned about
the dogs she'd adopted, the job she'd
never quit. They would replace her
after a few weeks of echoing absence near the meat slicer.

She did not want us to mourn, but to
pour out beers in celebration even if
she wouldn't be there to taste them, the hyssop-heavy
liquid thickened like a sauce that
we could use to baste all of our fears.

**Joe Baumann**
**St. Peters, Missouri**

# Emily's Virtues

Before her fingers lost
their cunning—my mother-
in-law, last of a generation
of refugees from up north—
we'd shell peas together,
culled from her yard,
our thumbnails
splitting the pods along
their green seams,
releasing the pale pearls
into an old enamel bowl,
the metallic *thunk*
a reward for the ultimate
virtue of diligence.

Another—thrift, her
unraveling and re-knitting
of old sweaters. And baking
into fresh bread my child's
leftover cereal.

Withered skin, yellow as
old linen. In her late
nineties, and her memory
slipping, she'd wake at
midnight, put on hat and
gloves, come down one
stair at a time, for church.
We'd lead her back
up to bed, wishing we had
her resolve, her faith
implicit that the way she
honored God, God would
honor her. Would hold on
to her the way she held

the banister, tight on the way
down, which was for her,
the way up.

**Luci Shaw
Bellingham, Washington**

## Little Leviathan

Beneath all the dithering, the beast of ages
gallumphs, wriggling hidden on seafloor fortitudes.

Tooth Cave of Writhing Flipper, it hunches
effortlessly indifferent like the pattern of gravity.

This exhausted tale has been hunted after
since Inuit spearfishers kept blubber lamps alight

on riffraff kayaks, bobbing amid icefloes.
Waiting for bubbles to surface, they sang

and chewed dried elk through the dream
sequence while narwhals mated and swam circles,

swung hipsongs beneath waxbright nightwater.
The most valuable piece of our earth may be

evidence of life which once existed,
the jewels and oils their bodies created

under tectonic pressure as fire and magma
shifted inside the doom core. I loved blizzards

as a youngster, smoking my own breath under a quilt,
belly full of boiled thyme and spitroast reindeer.

Beneath every warm bedding, the earthy beast
breathes fire, hiding in a dream sequence

like a valuable pattern—while our home-dome
became a frozen tomb we'd dig ourselves out of,

I made fantastic stories under my blankets.
Many-Headed Cavern with Ten Jaws,

Kayak Sinker and Hunter of Fathers,
God of Icefloes and Glacier-Maker,

Dream Whale: bless us with your fatty backside.
Bless us with your living, breathing breach

to this yak sky of quilted frost—we transform you.

**Forrest Rapier**
**Greensboro, North Carolina**

## watchclock (12/8)

where do you go
when Charlie
bends the air?

noir clubs,
heroin alleys,
stripper booths?

lamb island
or the sweatshop
haberdashery?

whiskey barrels,
candy plantations,
the monastery?

the 12/8,
you are what
moves the world,
keep bending the
soil's chemistry
with your
everlasting sincerity,
I hope
none of us
ever find you.

**Xavier Reyna**
**Harlingen, Texas**

## Folklore for Missouri Boys

Cut away the skin, bone, fat
of some dolphins washed ashore
and you'll find a boy nestled
in the slick, gray body.
Uncurling from sleep,
his eyes are dark as a deep sea vent.

We dress the boys in shirts and pants
and tell them how lucky
they are to have legs.
We send them into landlocked fields of grass
with hatchets and knives.
These boys, they only laugh when it rains.

These boys, they crouch low to watch
tadpoles at the creek, a sad hunger.
These boys, they long for salt and brine,
they fill their heads with water
and then they stumble home.
These boys, they kiss whoever's closest—

a body to rise against them like a tide,
its breath,
its fickleness,
and finally, after a storm: stillness.
These boys, they get married
and on weekends, they go fishing.

They bait their hooks
with skin and nails
like the water
might remember them,
like every sewer might be a way
back to the ocean.

**Kimberly Ramos**
**Kirksville, Missouri**

# Oscar, Gone Home Now

I had built myself a paradise just east of here, a mile
closer to New York where no one warns you to take care
of your teeth and where breakfast is always being made.

There in midmorning sunspots I escaped the boreal dark, north
a rewinding cassette of my great grandfather's voice left whirring
in a just sold car, north a quiet name said less often each year.

Childhood amnesia feels like what I imagine it felt like
back then to look out the airplane window, to try to see
patchwork through the nothing, to pull down the shade.

I fell west and sunsets came later, making shadow
puppets of Richard and Mary, their juniper canes.
I wanted to ask about the dog they used to walk.

I remember the sidewalk said Holly Is Loved
By Oscar. Eastwards I would picture them together
laughing as they approached the canvas of wet cement.

There are pomegranate trees gnarling in the alleyways
rooted in the pedestrian grout that bounds glazed places.
Twelve sweet bursts of bitter red keep me here in the West.

The dog is dead or else gone on to a better place, ran away
past a man crouched over hardening loss, roofing nail in hand
while I fly overhead two decades ago, squinting through the white.

**Phoebe Blake**
**Tucson, Arizona**

## The Teresa

The page never felt this good before
in my time at hospitals, the walls
                    white
suffocating me like a good way to die
almost like suffering
        memory rushing in
and then it doesn't.

    Nothing happens.
All you're left with is the skeleton
of your body and all that white bone.

Underneath a white bag, the page a paper bag
    containing the blue drink
                when it spills
almost your mother's apparition
          of Mama Mary
all blue inked veils and white marks like the
    whispers they don't tell you at the altar

On the white altar, the one you placed
sampaguitas in every Sunday, you were the one
who bought the flowers because Mama
couldn't walk, and you bought from the same girl.

And you were    that girl
the one selling ylang-ylang
        outside the church
and you were    that girl
inside your mother who could hardly walk
and you were    that girl
carrying your sling of flowers to Mama
hoping it would be a good offering
               a good sacrifice
you fist your knuckles    to God.

**Angela Gabrielle Fabunan**
**Olongapo City, Zambales, Philippines**

## On Edge

The Super calls me *Sweetheart* when I call him
for the leaking kitchen faucet, and the hundreds
of winged ants suddenly appearing on my windows
in early Spring. My name is Clementine, but he calls
all the women here *Sweetheart*.

Some day, I will move like a lizard,
corner him, pull out a chair, make him sit
and listen to the drip, drip, drip
into the night.

**Jerrice J. Baptiste**
**Kingston, New York**

# Plans

The benevolent leaves
sparkled, a high
definition green seemed to say, "Life is
too beautiful to leave
willingly." The wild clouds
crisp, and a blue
dream perfect
underneath a fixed sky,

rooted deep—and then, all
appeared ordinary
again, except
for the new memory abloom. Reluctant
to die, I await joy
in buds, in tumbleweeds.

**Dana Stamps, II**
**Riverside, California**

# Imagination at Reverie Lake

I

And sometimes
it finds us
like early morning
egret wings
pressing through
the fog—languid,
lowering, lifting.
Slender legs like
Snellen signs
center into view
and wait upon
that dewy log.
Bittersweet
scent of coffee.
Wings flick, head
sways. The egret
flits. Away.

II

Weeks, I wait. Weeks
watching
from the blind.
Hush. Here
it comes again.

III

Statuesque it stands
in the glass-like shallows
of Reverie Lake.
Head subtly bowed
and eyes softly closed
as if in supplication.
A celestial space
is made between

what is and what
we need to know.
Then slowly it moves
and dips its long beak
alone
into the light
—vanishing awhile
into itself. Concentric
circles swirl.

**Esther Palmer**
**San Francisco, California**

# The Crepe Myrtle Tree

I have read that we stay with our bodies
for three days after death.

When we viewed my father in his casket.
I saw his eyelashes move.
I told my husband.
He said he had noticed that too.

Listen: I have seen some of how we leave.
Go up, touch, come back.

Then on to exit:
One went through a hallway of stars.
One dropped a white rose as she left,
exclaimed it felt like Christmas there.
One was lifted among a million bubbles.
One cringed inside a cleansing light,
before being admitted.

I see my father in my vision, lighted
even under earth.
Body in place, not needed.
Free to go about the stars
with all knowledge of our universe.

He visits in my dreams.
We stand by a flowering tree.
He lets me know he understands our grief.
Takes a blossom, hands it to me.

**Linda Hughes**
**Punta Gorda, Florida**

# On the last day

we won't bowl.
I know you love it, the stiff shoes
and the smell of pizza and beer
and the pins reset again
and again and I'm sorry but
there is something about that weighted ball
that I can't let go of, my body
always wanting to follow it into
the gutter and the ground slippery
beneath me so that I can't stand
without seeking balance, there is
something familiar about that feeling that
I want to forget. The darkness
too deep to climb out of
and my fingers and wrists aching
with the pain of throwing too much away.

**s. Nicholas**
**Lake Arrowhead, California**

## parallelogram

the aftertaste of your worship
is a raw wound on the tongue
burning all you took with you to the earth
leaving me unable to taste whatever sweetness
remains in the far corners of this tilted room

i remember you standing 5000 miles away
in the dusty heat of a subterranean war
proclaiming your love in the voice of a
horseless don quixote as i lay half-asleep
shivering in the nakedness of winter

imagining you stepping over landmines
to send those words you had to say
i had to hear
the only gift you could give as you cheated death
to feed me the proofs of love

now i slide across my own desert
seeking those echoes i cannot taste
with my defective tongue every fruit
a dry ghost dripping nothing but sand
mocking me with the dazzling purity of loss

**RC deWinter**
**Fairfield, Connecticut**

# Professional Rioters

*While those who were arrested all live in Erie, we believe that there were professional rioters present from out-of-town because we overheard them asking for directions.*
    Dan Spizarny, Chief of Police, Erie, Pennsylvania

That's who smashed the coffee shop windows in Erie,
set the dumpster fires in Portland,
toppled the Confederate statues in Charleston.

As a professional rioter myself—proud member of the ARA
(American Rioter's Association)—I must confess
that not all of these uprisings are of our doing.

Rumor has it that there are some disgruntled school teachers,
some unhappy gas station attendants, a few radicalized
librarians, taking over their neighborhood streets.

Much as we professionals like to take the high ground,
I have to admit, some of these amateurs know how to hold
a sign, how to set a fire, how to pick up a stone.

Now, Officer, can you point me to that paint store again?

**José A. Alcántara**
**Carbondale, Colorado**

## Two Girls in Montana

Hot summer nights
    I played hurdles with you

Watching your figure ahead of me
    running with cool precision
    hands out, reaching
your small brown fingers would
    slap the head of the tall parking meter
    just at the moment
    your feet left the ground
    legs moving, angled outwards
        like wings
    slender arms pushing
    body pressed forward to sweep down
and hit the ground running
    your feet barely touching pavement
as you flashed to the next meter
    up and over

and on down the street
    meter to meter
framed by the light of street lamps
    and the muted glow from shop fronts

up and down main street
    we flew
    up and over, run…
    up and over

I followed you
    not as graceful,
    but followed
our faces grinning victory

we flew

**Judith Mikesch McKenzie**
**Eugene, Oregon**

## silhouette

kneeling        an archaeologist
mourns the present

a gentle brush undresses time
from an old skull

when does a life become a thing?

or its remnants art?

have faith       this hollowed out
fixed-stare vessel bathed in fresh light
once housed
      a concert stadium full of dreams
      whispered to a flicker
      in a night

ash for glitter

**German Dario**
**Tempe, Arizona**

# The Man in the Owl Costume

A potbellied man in an owl costume begins to speak
But the costume looks so real:
The eyes, black and glassy, empty
Of humanity, empty like an animal's eyes,
Cold dark deep and clear.
Moreover, his beak is too real. There is
No longer any evidence of a nose or mouth.
His looks like a mask worn by the
Kwakiutl Indians during a potlatch ceremony,
Where the one who sacrifices the most wins.
He looks like a fat old man wearing an Indian mask
That robbed him of his mortal spirit.
Just then a cat leaps down from the roof of a house,
A full story up, to catch a bird. But the cat is a house cat
& the man in the owl costume is a full-grown man.
I'm not sure what happens next. But a question
Occurs to me as the cat stretches out its body in midair:
Does the Kwakiutl Indian, after he's put everything
In the ceremonial fire, finally kill himself as well?

**Vincent Green**
**Santa Barbara, California**

# a harsh environment for our nature

when you see a butterfly for the first time
it will always be the first time.

my wanderer danaus plexxipus my
monarch. i reach my bouquet of salvia sylvestris
and attract
your orange hue to my may night sage. in full sun
we exchanged *i love you*. i'd cover myself in your
velvet and call my skin a map.
if eye contact were our only language
we could lay naked in the snow. watch it melt over
us and make winter re-think its timing.

but I woke dry, wilting my soft indigo over your
new yellow. not our yellow, dim yellow.
a reminder of orange and what
remains.

i became a child again, in a garden
with my hand out. i called to
each warm wind to every shade of you until
the last drip from my sweet-soaked hand
until a new season forced
me inside.

**Emily Jacko**
**Elizabeth, Pennsylvania**

# Protag

at the dentist the clock
is tooth-shaped and i feel ugly
in this communion
wafer light my tongue
thrashing is garbage
it's all Garbage.
I am just
Just feeling positively
*cratered* recently
wiggling
w all the peasants
@ the bus stop under the fat
lip of winter i know you want
the speaker of my poems
to have more agency but
if u knew me u would
just
*get it*
my aversion
2 vulnerability
the limp noodle
stuck in these 12 yr old
molars digging
    *digging*
it is all too raw
i wave
across the loud public
Parking lot in fear of the near
Distance between all living things i will
continue 2 live a private life
however sad
it makes me.

**grace (ge) gilbert**
**Pittsburgh, Pennsylvania**

# The city of diseased appletrees.

a view of broken buildings;
books on an unsorted
shelf. I love
these backsides
of houses—a chaos
of open windows, parked cars,
and felted roof
extensions, the garages, cemented
over cracks. water ingress crumbling
and drainpipes blocked
by rust. this city
of diseased appletrees
and bark knobbles.
floating brickdust
rising like heated
tobacco-smoke.
pillars of smoke
from gardens
of real tobacco.

**DS Maolalai**
**Dublin, Ireland**

# Autobiography

I am the tree that watched the grass mowed down:
Said nothing, did nothing, became nothing,
Because me they only clipped in places
And pruned to their tastes. I watched flowers drown
In the wind's rage, and went on whispering
Soothing nonsense to fill up the spaces
    In my dwindling canopy.

When the playing children watch the sky melt,
Its rumbling waters pierced with thunder
Over this most serene desolation,
They will not think of their own kind, but pelt
Storm and sky with abuse. They will wonder
When the zephyrs of their recollection
    Learnt to bring down a whole tree.

**Hibah Shabkhez**
**Lahore, Pakistan**

# Remainder

There comes a time when,
as if you have never thought
of it before, suddenly you see
the years ahead are fewer
than the years behind,
fewer days, fewer hours,
fewer springs, falls, less,
you realize, of everything,
and against all your wanting,
wanting not to,
you begin to subtract
the age you are from some
age that waits and you look
at that sum—
and whatever you do now,
whatever it is, you will think
there is something other,
something more,
you should be doing.

**Deborah Pope**
**Chapel Hill, North Carolina**

# Flock

They alight late,
swoop up wrapped
in scarves and shawls
all wrong
for hot September
breezes. They cheep
as they flitter
through the door,
just loud enough
for us to notice,
but not enough
for us to hear.

They observe us,
observing them,
then turn
in formation,
glide to the front
of the room,
assume a graceful
collective perch.
They've come,
they sing out,
to tell us about art.

Not art.

ART.

What art is.
What it can be.
How one can be changed by it.

They hang
their words around us,
watch us
for sudden moves.

Unseen bracelets
clank
and jingle.
Fringe and bell sleeves
waft down
like purple feathers.

I lose the thread
of their song,
mesmerized by their variations
on 1981's Stevie Nicks,
watch them wing
along the tailwinds
of their trilling
polyphonous anthem.

**Joey Brown**
**Loma Linda, Missouri**

## Concerning the Illegitimate Son of the Mayor from JAWS: Gov. DeSantis

------/\------

Florida dry humped
the movie JAWS,
and gave birth
to the Mayor's
bastard son.

He steals all our sunshine
and craps out
pathological Amity.
He fed us to the proverbial
political machine.

Unfortunately,
it does not have
the same theme music.

It swims in silence.

Open the beaches
and let's see those teeth!

The viral beast vs. the need to please
people and presidents.

The latter
swims in the same gene pool
as the great white privilege,
the ultimate apex predator.

Open the bars, strip clubs,
and make sure you brand
the teachers
with sanitized targets
when you force them

to swim
in halls of Petri dishes

where there is

NO

possible

way

social distancing
can change the fact

that there was never enough distance
between desks
and the dorsal finned
budget cuts.

This was no boating accident, Governor!

It was just you
enabling the contagions
to kill Summer, while she slept
and the holidays are next.

Throw more chum in the water
and wait for the moment
that you will, indeed,
need a bigger boat
to hide all your shame.

------/\------

**Christina Fulton**
**Hollywood, Florida**

## Legacy

I.
Your face is upturned,
chapped and peeling
in the sun.

Smoke billows from the grill.
You are surrounded by the scent
of burning flesh and wet hops.

Your voice roars, barreling
into the neighbor's
afternoon.

II.
I am terrified of driving.
I pass green Jeeps
and inspect each one.

I look for signs of you—
the bumper stickers,
the round face of rage.

My hands tighten on the wheel,
my vision blurs, I can't breathe, breathe,
breathe, please remember to breathe

III.
When I look at myself
in the mirror, your younger face
appears in mine, unexpected.

I recognize the features
from your high school photos,
now lost in a closet somewhere.

The short, dark curls crowning
dull blue eyes, mouth all yellow teeth—
your legacy.

IV.
In the dream, the walls and sheets
are white, glowing in buttery sunshine.
The only darkness is your hair, your eyes.

Your youthful body is feline-like,
you cross the bed,
assume the position of my lover.

Your familiar body against mine
creates the old heat.
Welcome back.

**Callie S. Blackstone**
**Connecticut**

# Drought

It hasn't rained here for a year
Fine dust is a matter of course
Sun slants off long rivulets of
Dry earth and brittle wind-blown grass

Clumps of spindly Black-eyed Susans
Hang their scorched heads, burnt and broken
A parched gray-green grasshopper sits
Reticent, sheltered by short shade

Perhaps tomorrow rain will come
Ragged and weak, needing practice
But for now, all that can be seen
Are faint clouds of hope in clear sky

**Margo L. Foreman**
**Lincoln, Nebraska**

## Rearview: Minnesota

the horizon is too far away; these flat lands swallow me
under cornfields, my body rots, feeding the cows of America
until I claw my way out, five years later; frozen ground cracks
   around me.
I admit it: I am no pioneer. the winds in this empty place have
   worn me raw
a century ago I would have given up the homestead and returned
   east,
defeated but relieved, never speaking of the fifty below days.
in the quiet left with five states between me and the ocean
I consider what silence and this emptiness has done to those
who first journeyed here, mostly norse, blonde, lutheran
how it has made them subtle, dangerous on the inside
wrapped in the non-threatening guise of bumbling skiers
easier to hide the knife-words in comical courtesy.
I, boston-born, do not belong here and having been beaten
I sigh, relieved, and point myself to a sea, any sea
where salt will heal and things are what they seem and feeling will
   come back into my feet
I am grateful for what I have learned here, though I think
I will never be able to speak it in words;
perhaps this is as it should be.

**Eve Taft**
**Castletroy, Co. Limerick, Ireland**

## Alternate Lives

Blond Donna, raven Harriet,
you both bathed unbeknownst
in diluvial longing, overflowing
from the moony homeroom boy
who'd scribbled hearts around your names,
penciled in between French declensions,
and roots of X.

That dry-mouthed boy in the corner,
who, at the bell,
never scrounged up nerve
to ask you out.

But in sundry universes of the infinite what-if,
smoother incarnations woo you both,
one whirlwind, one lasting years.
Each leads to union—house, kids, the works.

The tree of life keeps branching, though,
boughs for dove and crow alike;
Donna grows bored and leaves with both kids;
so I joyfully marry Harriet—
but her sudden death puts me on the skids.
Grief leads to downward spiral,
overdose, an orphaned son.

Meanwhile, a fool
in some backwater continuum,
goes on mooning
over what might have been.

**Michael Waterson**
**Napa, California**

# The Final Days of Houdini

My grandfather is drinking Canadian Club
as he stares at a birch tree
near the backside of the house.

He looks lost
but he isn't.

I tell him
"It's dinner time. Grandma's looking for you."

He grins
and holds up his whiskey.

"Let me dissolve this first."

He tilts his head back
with the glass to his lips
and I watch
as we both disappear.

**Chad Christensen**
**Omaha, Nebraska**

# Birth Duplex

*after Jericho Brown*

How do such small things excrete so much?
I joke that I'm an only mistake.

> I live with being an only mistake.
> Each night we choose upon whose sheets to slumber.

Each night we choose within whose tears to slumber.
I swallowed the tremor from the mountain.

> I swallowed from the tremor of the mountain.
> I can't uplift anymore. Quit needing me.

I can't uplift anymore. Quit kneading me.
Let me make my own biscuits.

> Let me bake my own biscuits.
> My antique soul in an app for that world.

We're antique souls in an app for that world.
How do such small things excrete so much?

**Jason A. Terry**
**Washington, D.C.**

## making a map

to dodge the broken bits of life that sigh too loud   when I wish for
    silence
some I couldn't love enough or with certainty
keys to those locks didn't fit        dropped haphazard in the dirt
phone calls never made couldn't bring myself to glue together
    words
cocoons more expedient wrapped in softness of nothing       no
    sound
crystal glasses dull in a glass cabinet never opened
    forgotten luggage I didn't unpack
ten tiny promises to myself        broken thought I'd get back in
    time  have another chance
some sagging balloons tied to a tilted mailbox        one went alone
    into the sky uncaring
weeds and uncut grass hide the path disappearing  from my feet
a wasp builds a nest       by the door
day fades again    solitary treasures torn and tossed along the way
the last photo gone        handwritten notes some sing some sting
    stories we should have told
but I don't always recognize       who wrote them
one silver ring you gave me as we walked   in the sunlight
so proud of your surprise I placed the unexpected joy curled
in the pocket of a sweater                I never returned
watching the dark yarn unravel uneven now        this is how the
    edges are

**Noël Bella Merriam**
**San Antonio, Texas**

## Handwringing Ridges

People stroke me like a worry stone
making pockmarked erosion
in my cliffs, the river below is not mine, nor are the people

It is hard to imagine the rubbing
Of human hands as something
beyond empty parentheses, hemlock, plutocracy

I loved hanging over parks
of lunching office workers, greenery
in people's voices, people named after white queens and kings

On a backwards road, I cross the bridge
children are in lines wearing uniforms
I look for floating bodies in the river, plastic bags and styrofoam in
    the brackish water

The river below is not mine, nor are the children, nor are the hands
    or the erosion
they've been taken from me
as the mother of everything, what hasn't

I don't get annoyed by ambulance sirens
or the moaning of drunk women having sex
the only real perversity that exists is monetary, fiscal depravity,
    unnatural revenue

That's what kills me, extraction, extortion
the children have words I don't know
I will catch someone looking at my colors, wanting to stroke,
    wanting to peel my eyes

With the tongues of my eyes, I taste
naturally reoccurring colors and in terror,
the knowledge of life from an unspiraling helix, a little apple, torn
    nebulas

I don't know how this works
there are handcuffs and clutching pearls
downcast eyes surround me

**Lily Rose Kosmicki**
**Denver, Colorado**

# Wash Day

The clothesline hums with the strumming of a spring breeze
till muted by hung-out sheets its song swapped for my mother's

humming of I'll Fly Away and the *thwack* of her shaking out
a wadded shirt or the *twang* of metal pants creasers

while semaphores of bleached underwear wigwag a counter lyric
and just inside the back door the wringer washer purrs and creaks

where she's added Cheer to the troubled water to wash away stains
and grime so we will be presented spotless at the front door

**Mark Rhoads**
**Lino Lakes, Minnesota**

# Clearing

*for C*

Every stone in my house
is stained with your beating heart—
the red ball you bounced
up & down the rooms

without a leaf
of sound

until finally growing tired—

> you slept
> in your mother's
> milk-stained shirt

> to be sent
> for washing

>> the next day.

**Trivarna Hariharan**
**Dwarka, Delhi, India**

# Elizabeth Bishop Reads My Horoscope

First things first,
move to Brazil.
No, that's second.
First get on a boat.

Tell yourself you are going on vacation.
Taste guava, cashew, mango, papaya.
The first act is to delude yourself.
Hope is a firefly constantly going out

and lighting up again. I never
mastered the art of postcards always
too many words to fit in one square.
I never wanted to drop it in the box

to surrender my words. My life—
one small postcard I kept
trying to rewrite while
drinking from a fountain of gin.

I never lost the right things.
Continents vanished,
but never my thirst.
Poems vanished

between the keys of my typewriter.
Losing, an art you can't help but paint,
absence always in the spotlight.
Maybe I should have sent those postcards

addressed but blank
desire's empty promises.
One day the mail just stops
return to sender.

Swallow another drink
or better yet, spit it out.
I made my escape through the bottle's
small neck but never managed to get out.

My miracles were burning
balloons falling from the sky
small animals fleeing
alone into black night

the way lips find each other in the dark.
or these words to your mouth.
Handwritten postcards yellow
hidden in a shoebox.

Better to write poems
even if you wrestle
the ending
for years.

**Julia McConnell**
**Seattle, Washington**

## Tattoo Days

On the road out front, a medium of exchange
comes and goes as it will. It's
a point of view, no, it's points of view
that keep our grammar in check.
I want mine to be more divulging,
or at least more intimate.
I want to fool around.

So Adieu! So long! I'm heading
in the directions of questions. Can
I levitate between beauty and truth?
Aren't I both subject and object? Aren't I
overwhelmed by what happens each day?

I remember those tighter times,
how I tried and tried to understand the given forms.
I felt cinched up. No pathos in that for me.
I couldn't keep it up.

The untidy sprawl beckoned
because it seemed more revelatory: I love
randomness because it gives a form all its own
like the prairie grass that finds its own way.

Heads still feel like exploding.
There's still work in quiet places.
And I've got this new tattoo!
Although it's quiet, it makes me feel.
All I want is it to feel.

**Dale Cottingham**
**Edmond, Oklahoma**

# Scorpinacity

For three days now I've been circling this scorpion.
In the morning, with incorrect eyes, I note its position,
say, three o' clock; by noon, it is at five. It flexes
its tail like an arm, a show of strength, the poison
in its sting just as painful, whether its dying or not, which
could be when it reaches seven or ten or tomorrow. By
evening I circle closer—a buzzard over this carrion. I think
this may have been the one that tapped my wrist in my sleep,
tattooing my veins red flames—watch the tail curl in
slowly, like a machine, then a dying breath
it unfurls; the click of the tip on the floor, an unsteady heart
rhythm. It will be days actually before it stops moving, and
weeks still before I sweep up its body.

My mother has surgery in five days. It could be her foot. Or
woman things. My sister knows the 6am intake schedule,
prepped her home for a three-week convalescent stay.
My sister will be the last face our mother sees, she will hold
our mother's hand, squeeze it, tell her we love her.
I have the will, and I stay where I am, three hours
away. Plenty of time, I think, for everyone to get to my mother's
side, I think, should I be called upon to do the one job my mother
wants me to do, knows I—and not my sister—can do.

**C. Prudence Arceneaux**
**Austin, Texas**

## salamander

spring and summer were spent tipping creek stones
ankle deep in the little sewage stream
behind my house. it had always *just rained*.
damp scalp-to-shoes, and in that tidal rush

blasting from the concrete pipe, i daydreamed
about amphibians. i believed frogs
perched on edges of every bank, i'd caught
half the toads in new england by that point,

though the salamander required more
labor, awareness. i only found them
after summer rain beneath bigger rocks;
even in perfect conditions, no catch

was guaranteed. redback salamanders
are the most common species: tiny, shy,
limbs like untied shoelaces. i captured
them by hand, looked into their kind faces,

let them traverse a landscape of fingers.
then, they'd crawl back into mud, their dark world
which was the same as mine: that remarkable
quiet, that wet air, oaks and waterbugs.

**Brendan Walsh**
**Hollywood, Florida**

## Bananas

I can't reach my oxygen mask. Blurry, I stretch
    toward yellow and white plastic dangling near me
but it's a banana hanging from an empty Wal-Mart sack.
    It turns brown as the tips of my fingers poke at it,

trying to get a grip. I read a poem about a boy
    revered by his friends for what he's able to lift
into his pockets from The Market Spot. The progression
    of lives transformed into familiar stereotypes

is poignant. It moves me. Two inches to the left.
    But I still can't reach the banana.

People around me crumble. But I'm mid-crumble too.
    My empathy is a tee-shirt worn into a cliche.
If I wash, rinse, and repeat one more Earth forsaken day,
    it will be reduced to a limp dust rag.

A basket of these rags grows in the laundry. If only I had energy
    to find the Lemon Pledge, I could restore this palace
to former glory—right at least one wrong
    as the world outside our door exercises its freedom

to self-decimate.

I notice a red triangle warning printed on the plastic
    but I can't read it. I must be dreaming.
I ask my partner if we have enough bullets for our gun.
    We might need to defend these bananas soon.

**Shyla Shehan**
**Omaha, Nebraska**

*Note:* The poem referenced in this poem is titled "Pockets" by Michael Torres posted online and promoted by poets.org on November 16, 2020, as part of the Poem-a-day series.

# When My Father Looked Up

When he looked up and said the sky
was thinking about rain, I turned my eyes
to the clouds, and there was the face
of the sky, its furrowed brow, pondering.

And in spring, when he said the fields were
throwing off their winter wraps, there were
the matted coats in the ditch. How had I missed them?
The dirty white scarves at the edge of the trees?

And when he said the woolly caterpillars
were predicting a bad winter, I saw them
gathered in council on the leaves of burdock,
black and orange striped, laying out the cards.

**Lucy Adkins**
**Lincoln, Nebraska**

## Deer Beds

This doe made it farther from the road than most—
back into the snowy woods
before the heart-shaped hooves
collapsed.

I stood by the carcass, frozen as she was,
thinking about the deer that emerge
from the woods at dusk into my backyard,
kneading the snow for corn
necks pumping at the slightest distraction.

Almost invisible at any distance—
their grey-brown coats the color of bark,
a camouflage against the brown fields,
but in the sprint across the road
they are as bare as panic.

I'll walk the woods again tomorrow,
and beneath the underbrush of clouds
pause where they sleep in auburn beds,
and know she is making her way
back to the woods.

**Jack Chielli**
**Frederick, Minnesota**

# Thirty-Six Zeroes

1.

Just a year ago
maybe two
I could answer all of her questions
besides the big one
*What happens when we die?*
now, I can answer
maybe half
she is quickening
I am slowing
soon we will pass each other
soon I will do the asking
and she, the answering

yesterday she asked me
how many atoms there are
in a drop of rain
I told her that I did not know
we looked it up
there are five sextillion atoms in a drop of rain
*How many zeroes there are in a sextillion?* she asked
we looked it up
there are thirty-six zeroes in a sextillion
*That's a lot of zeroes*, she said
I agreed

2.

we woke up to rain today
curtains, sheets of it
by the time we got to the race
a blue sky hung over the field
she stood there
in amongst them
younger, tiny
the pistol fired and they were off
she gave it her all

more even than we thought she had
finished fourth
afterward she came to us
wet and muddied
looked at us
tried to smile
and with my thumb I brushed away
the five sextillion atoms
that rolled down her cheek

**Steve Denehan**
**Naas, County Kildare, Ireland**

# Midnight's Fire

On that night, flames touched the sky
because the fire started on the second
floor and quickly spread to the roof.

Snow fell in dandelion-sized flakes
softly all the way down. It was enough
to leave a trail of blankets in the street,
but not enough to put the fire out.

The news van made it only minutes
after the fire trucks. Its tire treads
made patterns in the snow
like cable knit sweaters.

Their neighbors rushed to see the camera
crew, all padded coats and pajama pants.
Snow and soot sprinkled down upon them,
but in the flicker of red and blue lights,
the specks all looked the same.
Firework crumbs.

And as they watched the Yule log that
was their house burn into the night,
they thought about how cold the air
around them was, as the embers
and the stars looked the same too.

**Catherine Stansfield**
**Totowa, New Jersey**

## Eating the Last Tomato

Eating the last tomato of summer—
sliced and splashed with balsamic vinegar
and cold-pressed virgin olive oil—I think
of my father, who would indulge, at least once

each summer, in a bowl of sliced tomatoes
and red onions, dressed simply with red wine
vinegar and a pinch of sugar. *The way an old
Italian back home had taught me*, he would say.

The meal was completed by chunks of hearty
white bread to sop the juices, as all the while
he would proclaim: *I'm going to die of heartburn.*
He was close on that point; his heart failed.

I did not know then what heartburn meant.
Now, I do, and also the meaning of heartache.

**Kevin D. Norwood**
**Brentwood, Tennessee**

## Camping with Emily Dickinson

I dropped a white volume
whose pages were like glass
among some purple flowers...
in green and straw colored grass.

A leaf obscured the title.
A shadow crept over the spine.
And lives and lifetimes later
when I went to find a line,

I lifted a purple book up
from green, straw colored grass,
whose author was anonymous...
whose letters were like glass.

**William L. Ramsey**
**Greenwood, South Carolina**

Trust your instincts.

Subscribe to *Plainsongs*.

Please visit our website at corpuscallosumpress.com/plainsongs to subscribe via credit/debit card, PayPal, or check.

Our 2021 rates:
- One-year e-subscription ($10)
- One-year print subscription ($25)

Questions? Contact the editor at etucker@corpuscallosumpress.com or write to us:

Corpus Callosum Press
PO Box 1563
Hastings, NE 68902

CPSIA information can be obtained
at www.ICGtesting.com
Printed in the USA
BVHW091335110721
611330BV00001B/4